Prose and and Light

Zenobia Lundy

BK
ROYSTON
Publishing

BK Royston Publishing
Jeffersonville, IN 47131
http://www.bkroystonpublishing.com
bkroystonpublishing@gmail.com

Cover Design: Gad of Elite Book Covers

Paperback ISBN: 978-1-963136-97-5
Hardback ISBN: 978-1-963136-98-2
eBook ISBN: 978-1-963136-99-9

Printed in the United States of America

"You might be one person in the world,

But you can be the world to one person."

Zenobia

"I am no longer accepting the things I cannot

change.

I am changing the things I can no longer accept."

Angela Davis, A Political Activist

TABLE OF CONTENTS

PREFACE

The reoccurring theme of this collection is light. We all make choices in life. I think we can choose to have our light shine for all the world to see, or we can choose to live in darkness. The choice will always be ours to make. In a dark place, the light will guide us. The light will open our eyes at daybreak and light our path through all the midnights. The challenge is to find that light in our lives, wherever it may be, and hold on. For in finding that light we find our true essence for living.

As you read this collection, may you find your light and let it shine every day of your life.

THE PHOTOGRAPH

I wipe the dust away

Time and time again

And remember you

For all that remains

Is this frozen smile in time

We all become the photograph on the wall

Who will wipe the dust away for me

Who will look and remember

What mantel or nightstand will hold my smile

For I will someday become

That photograph on the wall

LIGHT

Let me be that light

Let me be that never-ending

Beautiful song that you hear

Let me that morning glow

That wakes you

And let me be that evening star

That sets your heart on fire

CHANGE

Light sparkled off the leaves as the sun entered her room

And her day began

She rose above the hate

She put the past behind

She wanted to change the world

She wanted to change her world

She realized that she was light

And she was beautiful

And she had changed the world

For she was light

And she was all

And she became

All the world saw, and it was beautiful

Dedicated to

Mrs. Michelle Obama

44th First Lady of the United States

BECAUSE I AM BROWN

Do you look away because I am Brown

Do you think I can't achieve because I am Brown

For all the times you ignored me because I was Brown

Did you not see me standing there

My heart aches sometimes because I am Brown

But I reached farther

And I stretched more

And I dreamed bigger

And I swayed smoother

And I sang louder

And jumped higher

And hit every ball harder

And hugged tighter

But most of all

I loved so much more

Because I am Brown

Let me be that light that inspires you

Moves you

And believes in you

Zenobia

LANDSCAPE

My landscape has no rolling hills
Or frothy ocean shores
The beauty it still has
In the path of memories it holds
Steps taken years before
On these sidewalks still
The small hands I held tight
And childlike memories
That line these streets for me
Of years long ago
When they were small
And I was young
Will forever be
The beauty in these streets for me
For every tree tells my story
And every crack I know

It's not so much what a man

says as what a man does

Zenobia

Amid the dreams of her past

I saw her fly with the wings of youth

She sailed from a land far away

Into a land of sugar cane and pain

She rose amid the hate

And never looked back

A distant dream

A home

THE POET

The poet lives between

A world of thought

And pen

A space of beauty and words

No paint

No clay

No canvas

That clear space

Is all an artist holds

SHE CRIED

She cried for the

        small things

The things that they left

        behind

The things that did not

        matter to them

All the things they did not see

        were the things she saw

She carried all the things

        they could not carry

For in her heart, she felt

        she must

She heard all the songs

        they could not hear

And in the end she felt all the Pain

BITS AND PIECES

Life is bits and pieces

Pieces of love

And pieces of sirens

Blaring in the night

Bits of stories of mayhem and murder

Of dreams at midnight

And tears at dawn

Loves lost

And loves found

Tomorrows and yesterdays

Bits and pieces of life

TO MR. CHAUVIN:

Why did you think no one would care?

Why did you think his life did not matter?

How dare you!

When you hurt one of us,

We all bleed

Whether you sit behind locked doors

Or one day walk free

You will always be a prisoner

A prisoner of that Memorial Day

A prisoner to screams

That pleading voice

Will ring in your ears for all your tomorrows

Colouring your days with regret

And shadowing your nights with tears

How dare you think his life did not matter!

FIRST LOVE

We all wonder about that first love

A blurry image of the man we remember

Where did the man go with the smile that melted my heart

His kisses were like fire

I would run a mile to see your smile

And stay up till the moon filled my world

To you, I was a girl

To her, you were a man

You made your way without me

And I never said goodbye

But somehow, you will always be my first love

Time and tide took you away from me

But maybe you wanted it that way

Maybe someday I will see your smile on the face of your

son

And maybe not

But I will always hold you deep in my heart

My sweet first love

Dedicated to My First Love

The faded faces of the past

Colour my tomorrows

And light the darkness of all my days ahead

I look back and smile and know

This is my life

My journey

My song

Zenobia

As a people

We have sought survival over justice

Longevity over vengeance

Silence over death

Zenobia

SILENCE

All good things are created in silence

Endured in silence

Maintained in silence

And like the

Morning Birds Song

Silence is to be savoured

Love me fiercely

With no regret

Love me hard

Love me for all times

Love me now!

Zenobia

In your quest for new things,

Remember to hold on tightly to the things

You already have.

Zenobia

OUR BLOOD

Our blood pours out of our hearts

Mixed with the tears of our mothers

From some endless stream of misery

It covers the ground

It covers cement

It covers tar

It covers grass

It pours out

It soaks through time

It pours out

Our blood

Like a sudden shower

On a sunny day

I packed my things

And rode away

I never looked back

I left all I knew

And all I had become

For a distant shore

For faces and places

I did not know

I left all the familiar

For all the unfamiliar

Zenobia

WINDOWPANE

A bed of silver blue

A shimmer in the wind

A reflection pool

Running down my windowpane

I see images in your pool of play

The skies open, and you wet all in your way

I thirst for you in the heat of the day

I listen for you in the night

Dripping on my paper, creating valleys as I write

A constant flow of life through my life

A sweet-salty taste upon my tongue

Life is short

Always sit in the most comfortable

Chair in the room

Zenobia

All that is given in love

Will forever bloom in the heart

Of the giver

Zenobia

In the end, it won't be the things you did

Or the mountains you climbed,

But the things you said

To the people you met along the way.

Zenobia

To be a woman

To be graced by God

To be the nurturer

To be the queen

The dancer

The lover

The one that gives birth

The one that lifts up

The one that cares

To be a woman

Is to be all of these

Zenobia

SMILED AGAIN

Nelson Mandela was imprisoned
But when he regained his freedom
He smiled again

Harriet Tubman travelled to and fro
For the freedom of her people
And in the end, she still smiled again

President Obama endured
was ridiculed, disrespected and hated
In the end, he smiled through it all

It is in our ability to endure
That makes it easy to always smile again

You cannot be what you cannot see.

Zenobia

GENUINE

To be genuine

Is to be all in

To be genuine

Is to let your eyes meet

And your heart speak

To really care

To listen

To show up

To make a difference

To smile

To speak

No price tags

No guilt

No hate

Just you

All in

Just for love

Just for life

LIKE A TREE

Let me be

Like a tree

Planted by the sea

Tall and strong

And anchored by my people

A link to the past

An ever-stretching limb to the future

Ever bending with change and time

Always there

Tall and strong

SOME THINGS

Are to be only remembered
And never repeated.
If we do not embrace our past,
We cannot move into our future.

LETTING GO

We let go of our children, our essence

For when we let go

Is when they truly begin to fly

We let go of our youth

For in letting go of our youth

Can we truly embrace our ageless beauty

And in the end

We let go of life

For all she was

And all we hoped she would be

When you need flowers in your life,
fill your vase with water.

Zenobia

I WAS

I was

The little girl

With ribbons and braids

And arms that wrapped around me

And tucked me in at night

I was

The young woman

With new loves who kissed me right

And lovers lost along the way

The woman I have become

With realities

And horizons of purple

And sunsets of orange

With brilliant days and navy nights

All I was and all I am

THE LADIES OF HILLSBOROUGH

I wanted to capture this slice of my life before time blurs it from memory. Time has a way of doing that. While living in Florida, I got a chance to volunteer at a women's prison about twenty miles outside of Tampa, Florida, in Hillsborough County. While attending a church service in Tampa, a visiting chaplain asked me if I would be interested in volunteering as a teacher once a week at a women's prison. I explained that I was not a teacher per se. She said that was okay; they needed someone to read with the women and encourage them. New to Florida and not really a highway driver, I took the prison address and said yes, I would try.

After filling out many forms and waiting for multiple background checks, I started volunteering at the Hillsborough County Women's Prison once a week every Saturday morning. The first time I drove there, I didn't have any idea where I was going. In the physical, I was lost and running on faith. I had to do this; they needed me. I didn't know what to expect that morning. It was a minimum-security prison that looked more like a college campus than a prison. And yes, I was a little scared; I've watched too much television, I guess. Like most things in life, it was nothing like what I expected. I anticipated the women would be hard, but they were warm and welcoming to me. They looked more like women who could have been schoolteachers, bank tellers, or even one of my aunts.

During the year that I went back and forth to that prison, I was changed. I learned so much about myself and the whole human experience. Sometimes in life, you stretch yourself, and yes, this was a stretch. I never missed a Saturday, not even one, because they were always there waiting for me, and I had no way to let them know I would not be there.

Many Saturdays, I cried when I returned to my car and looked back at the prison. I cried because I realized they were doing more for me than I could ever do for them. When you give of yourself, and your time, you become the recipient of the gift.

Every Saturday morning, I set out on a journey to teach them how to use writing to free themselves. I somehow hoped that through writing, they could find a release from their life of incarceration. Many of them did enjoy the art of writing. That part of my journey is reflected in many of my poems.

For a few hours over the course of a year, I got a glimpse of how it must be to lose your freedom.

Sometimes, I would bring newspaper clippings or perfume samples. I became their link to freedom and the world they had left behind. No matter what the weather was or if I was late, I always found them there waiting for me. We had a regular classroom with tables and chairs lined up neatly. I was their Saturday morning teacher.

Florida allowed open access to prison records; you could find out the offense that led to incarceration. I never went online to find out the whys. I always wanted to see them as people and women who had made a wrong turn on their journey.

I was not a published author during this time, but I was always writing. They were the earliest supporters of my writings. We wrote a small book together, and they all contributed their writing, which was one of our projects. We read together, and I am sure we grew together.

I had to return to Philadelphia unexpectedly. I let them know that soon, it would be our last Saturday together. My previous Saturday with them was bittersweet, for we all knew it would be our last Saturday together, but our time together would last a lifetime in our hearts. They gave me cards, blank journals, artwork, smiles, and as much of themselves as possible. I reminded them that "wherever I was and looked up into that nighttime sky and saw the moon, it would be the same moon they would be looking at, and we would always be forever connected." Those are the words I left them with our last Saturday together.

I often think of the ladies at the Hillsborough County Women's Prison and believe in my heart that each one has found her way.

You can be one person in the world and be the world to one person, and on those Saturday mornings they were my world.

From the pain

Came a song

From the tears

Came life

We fought

The fight for life

And we won

Zenobia

THE LITTLE THINGS

In every puddle, there is a ripple

For every teardrop leaves a stain of remembrance

And all the days gone by

Will fade with time

And tomorrows will come

Like sunrises in the morning sky

Ever new

OUR PEOPLE

Our People
So deep and dark
Like the ocean

Our People
So warm
And golden
Like the sun

THINGS 2

I have no room for things
They seem to crowd my very being
The space they occupy
Seems to take away from my space
For somehow, they upset me now
For now, I know they will exist
When I am no more
I will be gone
And they will remain
How dare they!
I have no more room for things
Well, maybe just a few

A LIGHT

You must be still

To hear the moon

Go from half to full and back again

To see the trees drop leaves of summer's child

And if you look into a child's eye

You will see a light

A gentle light

A light you cannot touch

A light from a special place

A light that grows deeper and richer with time

It is of no value to learn what is right,

and then not do what is right.

Zenobia

The constant chatter
Of death will always
Surround us

Zenobia

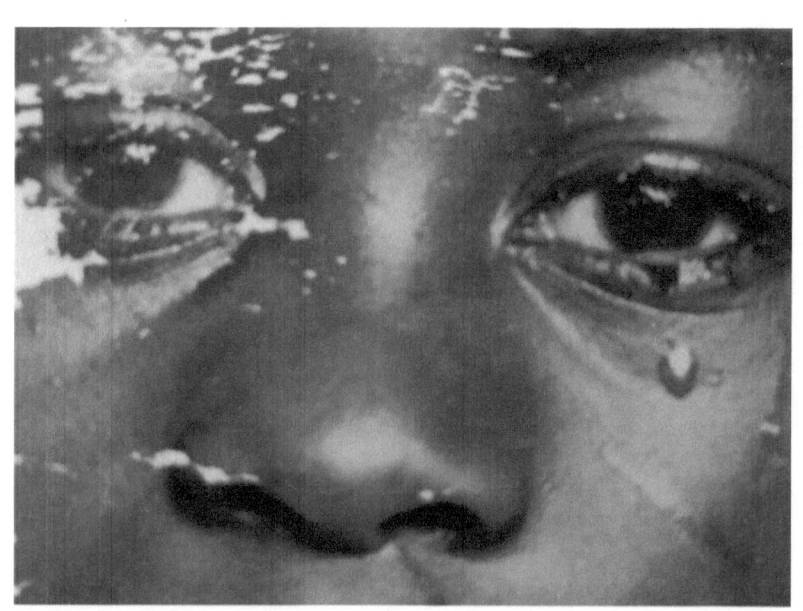

TWENTY LITTLE PIECES

I did not know you

I had not touched your hand

Or wiped your mouth

Or held you in my arms

When you were sick

Or seen you laugh and play

But the mother in me

Has a broken heart for you

I cried for you today

So much life ahead

But today, you play with angels

And you dance among the stars

And today

Twenty little pieces of my heart

Were chipped away

And will always miss you

For you are every child

And I am every mother

And today, I cried for you

Dedicated to Every Child of War in the World

Do we all not long for the past

Do are hearts and minds seek out the way it was

But time heals broken hearts

And life belongs to the living

For time will catch us all

And we will become like the leaves in winter

Zenobia

LOVING SOMEONE

Too much energy

Too much talk

Too many tears

Too much time

Too much trying

To read between

The lines

You gotta live

You gotta Dance

Headlines are scary

Life is Short

You gotta live

You gotta Dance

Zenobia

CHOICE

The greatest evil

Is when we convince ourselves

We have no choice

The choice cannot be taken

The choice comes from within

And the choice always belongs to us

I write so

I can breathe

And I breathe

So I can write

Zenobia

OUR HAIR

We tease it, we freeze it

We shape it, we bob it

We do-rag it

We shag it

We curl it, we conk it

We twist it, we braid it

We make it purple

We make it pink

We wrap it, we plait it

And

We dare *anybody* to say anything about it!

The pinks of morning glow

That blanket each new day

That shimmers

Across water

And fades

From a deep place

Zenobia

If I could give you a ladder to the future

I would help you climb

I would let you know you could be a leader

Because, you once were a king

Zenobia

TIME

The pile of New York Times I keep beside my bed

The unread books that stare me to sleep each night

All remind me of time

How time is no friend

She marches forward

Like some breath, some energy

We dare to touch

We try to grasp her

For she forever slips away

Into our dreams

And into each new day

PRINCESS

She walks like a princess

With eyes shining like jewels

Her court surround her

She comes from a great history

A noble past

Her belly swollen with dreams

The winds of change

Blowing all around her

In her eyes, I see a child

The child of yesteryear

In a belly swollen

A dream deferred

A baby too soon

A woman too late

It's not what could have been

Or what should have been

Or what might have been

But what is

Zenobia

SISTAS

Yeah, they talk in Ebonics
F___ this and F___ that
My sistas of these concrete streets
Tight braids and tight jeans
Swollen bellies
From leftover nights of passion
Designer bags in ghetto rooms
And babies' daddies on
Airbrushed hands
Forgotten dreams
Line the hearts
Of my sistas
From these concrete streets

Young men become old men

And flowers will fall away

And all that was

Will fade

Birds will always fly

And love will turn

And life will always begin again

Zenobia

If we do not embrace our past,

we cannot move into our future.

Zenobia

There is never a river so wide,

that a smile cannot shorten.

Zenobia

Growing up Black in America

Is not merely, having grown up

But to have survived

Zenobia

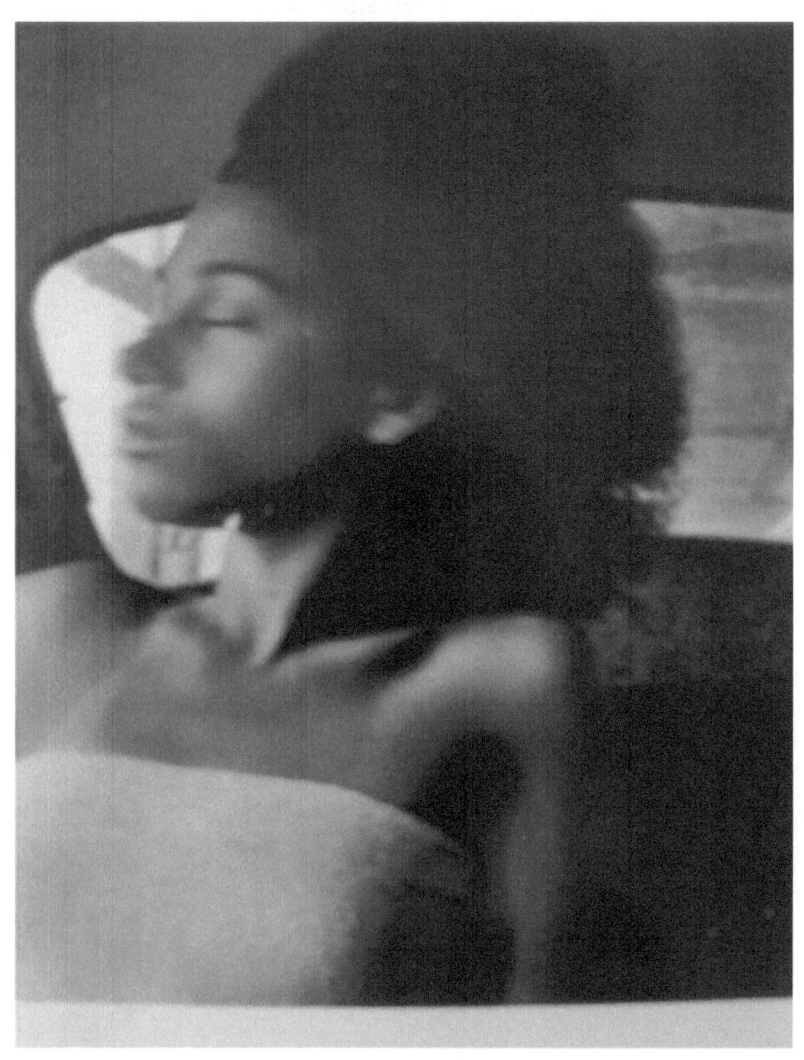

PAST LOVES

She drank Fiji Water

And smoked French Cigarettes

And you will always remember how her Jeans fit

And you never knew what she was thinking

And you were always too afraid to ask

And you will always remember how she smelled

Like Morning Dew

At Midnight

THESE ARE THE TIMES

Little Girls with Big Dream

And Old men with Big Regrets

Color my Days

And Shadow my thoughts

Unjust Laws.......

Apathy Abounds......

Guns for Sale....

Land of my Birth....

Godless

Lawless

These are the times

LET ME GO

Let me go

Let me slip away

Let me go into air

Let me visit you

If only in your dreams

Let my smile

Dance with you

In all your tomorrows

Let me go

We as a people have maintained our humanity,

Amid massive inhumanity

Zenobia

We all possess the ability to endure

That boundless spirit of endurance

We endure beyond our thoughts

Beyond our expectations

Beyond where our mind takes us

Beyond here

Zenobia

However, humble our circumstances,

Undramatic our talents, our true purpose has been revealed.

We were meant to be this person at this time and place

Not for ourselves, but for other people.

We were meant to make this contribution to the world.

And so, we must do it well,

Do it with faith and patience,

With all our strength and passion,

And in doing so, discover who we really are.

Marjorie Holmes

ACKNOWLEDGEMENTS

First and foremost, I give thanks to my heavenly father who has guided me on this beautiful journey called life. I give thanks to my ancestors who dreamed so I could fly.

I give thanks to my family in the Carolinas who inspire and support me across the miles,

To my dear friend and Dance teacher Nicole Rodriquez, whose phrase "keep your eyes on your own paper'' I continually repeat in my head, reminding me, that this is my journey, my dance, my life, and never look to the right or left, but straight ahead.

To my friend Deidre Farmbry whose smiles and support has meant so much to me during the writing of this book.

To my sister Kathleen who always knows how to take me away from it all and just have fun.

To Jon Batiste whose music over the last year became the soundtrack of my life, allowing me to write and listen to music at the same time.

To my dear children Jasmine, Thomas and my grandson, Camryn who constantly remind me of how much I am loved.

Let me not forget my rock, my husband Bill, who is my constant support and light through all the seasons of my life.

To my Editor who listened to all my ideas about this book and about life.

Thank you Julia.

ABOUT THE AUTHOR

Zenobia Lundy was born in Philadelphia Pennsylvania and educated in Philadelphia. This is her second collection of Poetry. Her first collection of Poetry is entitled *Reflections of Us*.

She travels the country doing Book Fairs and speaking engagements. She enjoys reading her Poetry to live audiences. Zenobia is a lifelong Poet, just recently entering the realm of publication. Her work has appeared in Drexel's University's *Writers' Room 2024 Anthology* Edition, in Philadelphia.

She continues to be inspired by life in the urban environment in which she lives.

Zenobia is currently completing her Bachelor of Arts degree in Creative Writing at Rosemont College, and lives in Philadelphia with her husband Bill and their cat Lucky. She can be contacted and her books can be purchased via her Website: www.Zenobiathepoet.com

www.ingramcontent.com/pod-product-compliance
Lightning Source LLC
Chambersburg PA
CBHW020332130626
46549CB00003B/1149

* 9 7 8 1 9 6 3 1 3 6 9 7 5 *